The Banking Business

Henry Allen

Copyright Page

Publisher: Univon

Index

Banks Don't Sell Money, They Sell Debt

Have you ever wondered how banks make money? At first glance, it seems like they sell money. They lend you a certain amount, and you pay them back with interest. End of story. But that's just the surface of the game. The truth is, banks don't sell money; what they really sell is debt. And that little detail changes everything. It changes how you see them, how you relate to them, and, most importantly, how you can use them to your advantage to become rich if you understand the rules well.

When someone thinks of a bank, they often imagine a place where you keep your money for safekeeping. But that's an illusion. What you're really doing when you deposit money in a bank is lending it to someone else. Yes, the bank doesn't keep your money in a vault waiting for you to need it. It takes it, multiplies it, and lends it to others. And it doesn't lend it just once; it lends it many times. The system that allows this is called "fractional reserve." Simply put, if you deposit $1,000, the bank is only required to hold a small fraction—say, $100—and can lend out the other $900. But the interesting thing is that that borrowed money goes back into the system. If the person who received the $900 deposits it in another bank, that new bank can keep only a portion and lend out the rest. So, suddenly, that initial $1,000 turns into $10,000 or more in loans. The bank has created new debt out of thin air, simply because someone trusts the system and leaves their money there.

This isn't bad; it's simply how it works. The problem is that no one explains it to you this way. No one tells you that when you go to ask for a loan, you're not buying money, you're buying debt. And that debt is a product. One that is packaged, sold, resold, insured, and even transformed into financial instruments for investors around the world. For the bank, you're not a person who needs financial help. You're a customer who's buying a product: a debt that you'll generate with your monthly payments, and that, if you do it right, will pay much more than you borrowed. For the bank, that stream of payments is what's valuable.

Imagine a bank lends you $100,000 to buy a house. You think they've done you a favor. But it didn't cost the bank anything to create that money. They just put it in an account and that's it. And you, with a lot of effort, will spend the next 20 or 30 years paying it back, plus another $50,000 or $70,000 in interest. For the bank, that loan was a brilliant business. They didn't sell something tangible. They sold a promise: the promise that you'll go into debt with them and make payments for decades.

That's why banks love responsible debtors. Not those who have a lot of money and don't need loans. They make money from well-managed debt. They're more interested in someone who borrows and pays than in someone who never borrows. And this is where the opportunity comes in for those who want to use the bank as a partner, not an enemy. If you understand that what they're selling is debt, you can start buying that product strategically. Instead of borrowing money out of necessity, you do it intelligently: you take on good debt that earns more money than it costs. And so, instead of working to pay off debt, you make the debt work for you.

Think of it like an entrepreneur. Imagine you can borrow $200,000 from the bank and use it to buy properties that generate monthly rental income. If that income exceeds the monthly loan payment, you're winning. You didn't use your money; you just used the product the bank sells: debt. You bought debt, but you transformed it into income. And the best part: the bank is happy because you're paying every month. To them, you're an ideal customer. But you also win. It's a win-win relationship, if you know how to play the game.

The problem is that most people only see debt as something negative. Because that's how we were taught. Debt is bad, we were told. But that's because most people don't know how to use it. It's like fire: in the hands of a child, it can be dangerous. In the hands of a chef, it creates wonders. If you use debt to buy liabilities, like new cars or trips, you'll sink. But if you use debt to acquire assets that generate money, you're taking advantage of the exact same system that makes big business owners and investors rich.

Banks thrive on debt. They thrive on people who make their payments every month. So, every time you take out a loan and pay it off, you become more valuable to them. Your credit history becomes a calling card. And if you learn to present yourself as a reliable investment for the bank, the bank will give you more. It will see you as someone who can buy more debt. And every time you buy good debt, you'll be using the bank's business to grow yours.

So, stop thinking of the bank as a place to keep your money or to borrow when you're in trouble. Start thinking like an investor. View debt as a product. One you can buy wisely, and one that can help you build wealth if you know how to manage it. The bank doesn't lend you money out of pity; it does so because you're buying the product they're selling. And if you learn to resell that product in the form of income-generating assets, you'll be playing the game by its own rules.

Always remember this: the bank makes money because it sells debt. And you can make money if you learn to use that debt as a building tool, not a trap. Don't buy things that don't make you money. Buy debt only when you can use it to produce more than it costs you. That's how rich people think. That's how banks operate. And that's how you, too, can start playing on the same team, but with your own goal: to get rich.

What Do Banks Really Do With Your Money?

When you take your money to the bank and deposit it into an account, you think it's just sitting there, patiently waiting for you to withdraw it. You imagine it's stored in a safe, or at least on a computer with your name on it. That's the image we all have when we think of our bank accounts. But the reality is very different. Once the money enters the bank, it's no longer there as you think. It's not sitting there or waiting. It's being used. It's being multiplied. It's working... but not necessarily for you.

To understand what banks do with your money, you have to imagine something closer to a trading floor than a vault. The bank takes the money you and millions of others deposit and turns it into its raw material. It doesn't just leave it sitting there. It lends it, moves it around, and reinvests it. That money becomes the bank's foundation for making money. They don't get rich off deposits alone; they get rich because those deposits allow them to make more loans. And each loan generates interest, fees, and more business. That's the real source of bank wealth.

The system that enables all this is called fractional reserve. It's a technical concept, but let's make it simple. It means that the bank isn't required to hold all the money you deposit with it. It only needs to hold a small fraction, a kind of mandatory "buffer." For example, if you deposit $1,000, the bank might be required to hold only $100. It can lend out the other $900. But the interesting part doesn't end there. Because when someone borrows those $900 and deposits them in another bank, that second bank does the same: it keeps a tiny fraction and lends out the rest. And so on. With that same initial money, banks can create multiple loans, over and over again. In short, they're creating new money based on debt, not real money.

This process is completely legal and is part of how the modern economy works. It's what makes credit available to buy homes, finance businesses, or pay for college. But it also means that banks don't have all your money physically available. If all a bank's customers went on the same day to withdraw all their money, the bank would collapse, because it doesn't have it. Not because it was stolen, but because it's borrowed, invested, or circulating elsewhere. Your money is scattered in bits and pieces everywhere.

In addition to lending money, banks also invest it. They buy bonds, stocks, and financial instruments. They look for opportunities where they can earn a return. Your money becomes just another piece on the bank's investment board. They make decisions with it, always with the intention of making more money for themselves. They pay you minimal interest for having it there, if they pay you anything at all. But in return, they're using it to generate much higher interest through loans, mortgages, credit cards, and financial products for other customers.

And here's another important point: the bank doesn't tell you exactly what it does with your money. You can't choose whether your deposit is used to finance a house, a business, or a stock market investment. Once you hand it over, you lose that control. But what you can do is understand that the bank is making money from it. A lot of money. They profit from your inaction. While you have your savings account as a kind of cushion just in case, they are using that cushion to build financial buildings that generate millions.

That's why banks always encourage you to leave your money with them. They offer security, convenience, and easy transfers. They give you a card to make you feel in control. But the real control lies with them. Your money is their fuel. And the more fuel they have, the more they can grow, lend, and invest. In fact, within the bank's structure, deposits are viewed as liabilities, but also as powerful tools for generating assets. It's an accounting game that allows them to win as long as public trust is maintained. Because that's the only thing that sustains this entire system: trust.

When you know all this, your relationship with the bank changes. You understand that, even though they seem to be looking after your money, what they're really doing is using it for their own purposes. That's not wrong. It's their business. But you, too, can learn to play this game. You can stop seeing the bank as a guardian of your money and start seeing it as a partner from whom you can benefit. You can learn to take out loans that earn more than they cost, just as they do with your deposits. You can create your own strategy where the bank serves you, not the other way around.

The key is to stop being passive. Stop thinking that having money in the bank is the goal. Keeping it sitting there only benefits one person: the bank. You don't get rich off it. What enriches you is knowing how money moves, how banks use it, and how you can do the same. And it all starts by understanding this basic principle: the bank doesn't keep your money, it puts it to work. But not for you. It does it for them. Unless you learn to do the same.

So, the next time you deposit money, do so knowing that you're participating in a system where your money becomes a tool. Think like an investor, not a mere saver. Observe how the bank makes money, and copy its model. You don't need to be a millionaire to get started; you just need to understand how money really moves behind those glass and marble doors. Because once you understand that, you can stop being just a customer... and start playing like a true partner.

The Hidden Power of Financial Leverage

Most people grow up with the idea that to make money, you first have to have money. They teach you that you must save, work hard, and gradually build your wealth. And while that mentality has some truth to it, it also has a huge limitation: it's slow, and in many cases, insufficient. Because in a world where prices rise, where opportunities appear and disappear quickly, saving to invest can take years, while others are already building empires. The difference? They use a tool that seems magical, but isn't. It's called financial leverage.

Leverage is simple to understand: it's using other people's money to grow your own. And the best example of how it works is found in banks. They thrive on leverage. They use money that isn't theirs—the money of depositors—and lend it out with interest, over and over again. But here's the interesting part: you can do the same thing. You can use the bank's money to build your business, buy a property, or finance an investment that will earn you more than the loan costs. Instead of working years to raise capital, you can access it intelligently and make it work as if it were your own.

Imagine this: You want to buy a property that costs $100,000. You could spend years saving, cutting expenses, and sacrificing your lifestyle to get to that figure. Or you could use leverage. You take out a loan from the bank, put down 20%, and finance the rest. That means with just $20,000, you can control an asset worth $100,000. And if that property rents for more than you pay the bank each month, you're already generating income. You're using other people's money, not your own, to build wealth. That's the power of leverage. It multiplies your possibilities without needing all the capital.

Now, it's important to clarify something: leverage isn't magic. It's not something that just works. It's a tool, and like any tool, misused, it can cause damage. That's why many people are afraid of it. Because they've seen cases where debt becomes a burden, where interest eats into income, where risks turn into losses. But it's not the fault of leverage. It's the fault of not knowing how to use it. It's like a kitchen knife: in the hands of a chef, it creates incredible dishes. In inexperienced hands, it can cut where it shouldn't.

The secret is to use leverage only to acquire assets that generate money. Never to buy things that lose value. You don't take out a loan to buy a luxury car that depreciates in value. You take out a loan to acquire a property that pays off every month. You don't use your credit card to go on vacation, but to finance inventory you know you'll sell at a profit. Smart leverage allows you to earn more than the debt costs you. And when you achieve that, it doesn't matter if the money isn't yours. The return is yours, and it's real.

There's something powerful in this idea: you don't need money to start building wealth. What you need is access to capital and a solid plan to use it well. And that's exactly what great entrepreneurs do. How do you think shopping malls, buildings, and chain stores are built? It's not with money saved for decades. It's with leverage. It's loans, investors, banks, funds. It's borrowed money, strategically placed to multiply. And if they can do it, you can too. You just need to think like an entrepreneur, not an employee.

And this is where many people fall behind. Because they're so used to working for money that it doesn't occur to them that money can work for them, even if it's not theirs. They believe borrowing money is only for when you're in trouble. But the rich don't see it that way. They borrow money when they see an opportunity. They don't fear debt if that debt is tied to income. They know that the interest they pay is the cost of accelerating growth. And they'd rather pay that cost than wait 10 years to have the necessary capital.

Furthermore, leverage has a multiplier effect that savings can never give you. If you invest your $20,000, you might make a small profit. But if those $20,000 allow you to control a $100,000 asset, and that asset appreciates or generates income, your profit is much greater relative to what you invested. That's the key. You're generating a return on something larger than your initial investment. It's like using a lever: with little effort, you can move something much heavier. That's where the name comes from.

But be careful, this requires discipline and vision. You can't make the mistake of leveraging without knowing what you're getting into. You can't take on debt just because it's offered to you. You have to calculate, plan, and assess risks. You have to learn to think like banks: Will this money I'm going to lend me return more than it costs me? If the answer is yes, go ahead. If the answer is no, then you're not ready for that move.

In the end, financial leverage isn't really a hidden secret, but it is a hidden power for most people. Because it's not taught in school. It's not explained to you at home. It's knowledge that those behind big projects have. And now you can have it too. You don't need to wait until you have a lot of money to get started. You just need to understand how to use other people's money to build assets that work for you. Because if there's one thing you should remember, it's this: money has a cost, but it also has potential. And if you know how to use it well, that potential can change your life forever.

The Rich Client vs. the Poor Client

In the banking world, not all customers are the same. Although we can all walk into a branch, open an account, and receive a smile from the teller, the truth is there's a huge difference between how poor and wealthy customers are treated. It's not just a matter of money in the account; it's a matter of how each person uses the bank, how they understand it, and how they turn it into a tool. While poor customers see the bank as a place to keep their money, wealthy customers see it as a strategic ally to multiply it. That difference changes everything.

Poor customers usually have a savings account, a debit card, and perhaps a credit card with a small limit. Their relationship with the bank is one of respect, sometimes fear. They have the mentality that going into debt is dangerous, that it's best not to owe anyone anything, that saving is the safest option. They deposit their salary, pay their bills, and try not to use their credit card to avoid interest. If they do ask for a loan, they do so with fear and pay it off as quickly as possible because they believe debt is a trap. Their goal is to be "up to date" and avoid problems. But they rarely use the bank to advance financially.

The wealthy client, on the other hand, has a completely different relationship. He doesn't deposit his money to keep it "safe," but to move it. He has interest-bearing accounts, mutual funds, lines of credit, multiple cards, and, above all, he has access to large-scale financing. But the most important thing isn't what he has, but how he uses it. He knows that the bank is a source of cheap money if he knows how to use it. He knows that going into debt isn't bad if that debt finances something that generates more money than it costs. The wealthy client takes out loans, not to survive, but to multiply. And that makes him a partner of the bank, not a mere user.

There's one key thing that wealthy clients understand: banks want clients who make them money. Not clients who simply save their paychecks each month. That's why, when a wealthy client requests a line of credit, the bank prioritizes them. They offer lower rates, more flexible terms, and personalized advice. Not because they're a good person, but because the bank knows they'll make a profit with that client. They're clients who move large sums, who borrow and repay, who invest, who make their money grow. And the more they do this, the more doors open.

On the other hand, the poor customer, even if they're punctual, even if they're never late, doesn't generate significant profits for the bank. In fact, they're often charged for having their account, for using it, for making transfers. They're offered loans with higher interest rates, cards with annual fees, and commissions on almost everything. The system is designed so that those who don't know how to use it pay more. And the saddest thing is that these customers often believe they're acting responsibly, when in reality, they're trapped in a cycle where they'll never grow. They're paying to use the system, while others make money off of it.

The difference between these two types of clients isn't the amount of money they started with, but their mindset. The wealthy client studied how the financial system works. He learned to play the bank's rules to his advantage. He understood that having access to credit is an advantage, not a burden, as long as it's used wisely. He saw that he could build assets with borrowed money, and that the income from those assets could pay off debts and leave him with a profit. He didn't focus on not owing anything; he focused on building something that would allow him to live better. He used debt as a tool, not a threat.

The poor customer, on the other hand, often repeats ideas they've heard from others who were also trapped. They believe that all loans are bad, that rich people are rich because they were born lucky, that saving is the only sure way to get ahead. And that way of thinking keeps them small. Even when they have leverage opportunities, they reject them out of fear. Even when they have access to a card or credit, they misuse it, buying things that don't generate income. And then they complain about the bank, failing to see that the problem isn't the institution itself, but rather their lack of knowledge of how to use it.

But the most powerful thing about this comparison is understanding that anyone can change their mindset. You don't need to be born rich to think like a rich person. You can start today studying how finance works, how banks operate, how to use debt to generate income. You can begin to view your bank account as a tool for growth, not a safe. You can stop fearing credit and learn to use it to your advantage. You can become a customer the bank seeks out, a customer they value, because they know they'll win with you. And if you win too, then it's a powerful relationship.

The truth is, banks don't differentiate based on friendliness. They differentiate based on profitability. And you can become a profitable customer if you stop thinking like someone who saves money and start acting like someone who makes it grow. Changing your relationship with the bank means changing your relationship with money. And when you do, you're no longer a spectator of the financial system. You become an active, strategic player who knows how to move forward. And that, in the real world, makes all the difference between continuing to survive... or starting to build wealth.

How to Make the Bank Work for You

Most people think they work for the bank. They work to pay their mortgage, their consumer loan, their credit card. They strive month after month to stay on track, to avoid falling behind, to avoid high interest rates and collection calls. It's as if the bank were their silent boss, the one who tells them how much they can spend, how they should live, what they can and can't do with their money. But the truth is, there's also another way to live: making the bank work for you. And that, although it seems remote, is entirely possible if you understand the rules of the game.

First, you have to understand that the bank is a tool, not an enemy. It's not just made to charge you; it's also made to help you grow, if you know how to ask for it. The bank has a resource you can use: money. And it's willing to lend it to you if you meet certain conditions. It's like a partner who can finance your ideas, your businesses, your investments. But, like any partner, it won't do it out of charity. It wants you to win, yes, but only if it means it will also win with you. So the key to making the bank work for you is to offer it a solid reason to trust you.

One of the most common mistakes is seeing the bank as just a place to keep money. You deposit your paycheck, withdraw cash, make payments, and nothing else. That's like having an expensive computer just to use as a calculator. The bank has financial products, tools, and access that can completely change your financial situation if you know how to use them. You can access loans for investment, lines of financing to grow your business, and mortgages to acquire properties that generate monthly income. But to get there, you must build a relationship with the bank. It's not about getting on the manager's good side; it's about building a track record.

How do you build that relationship? With strategy. Open a checking account if you don't have one yet. Use a credit card, even for small amounts, and always pay it on time. Show that you know how to manage your money. If you have a stable income, declare it, record it, make it visible. All of this makes you a trustworthy customer, and banks love trustworthy customers. Within a few months, you can start requesting credit increases, new lines of credit, even a small loan. Not to spend on worthless things, but to invest in something that will give you back more than what you paid.

Let's say you have a small business. You can use the bank to grow it. You don't need to wait until you have all the money. If you can prove your business is generating revenue, that it's real, that it's operating, you can apply for a loan to expand. Perhaps buy more inventory, improve your premises, invest in advertising. And if that loan generates more sales, then the bank literally worked for you. It lent you money, you multiplied it, paid off the debt, and also kept the profit. That's using the bank as a lever for growth, not as a burden.

You can also do it with real estate. Instead of saving for years to buy a house, you can use a mortgage. The bank lends you the money, you make a down payment, and you buy a property. If that property rents for more than you pay the bank, you have passive income. And the best part is, you didn't put up all the money. The bank did. It worked for you. Sure, you did the analysis, took the risk, managed the investment, but the initial money came from somewhere else. That's the difference between thinking like a consumer and thinking like an investor.

Another way to use the bank to your advantage is through negotiation. Most people don't know that banks are willing to negotiate. If you're a good customer, you can ask for better rates, eliminate fees, extend terms, and even restructure your debts under better terms. But you can only achieve that if you know what you're doing, if you know your rights, and if you've built a good reputation with them. The bank, like any business, wants profitable customers. If you prove that you are, they'll treat you as such. And then doors that seemed closed open.

Something important you need to understand is that banks don't create money. The money they lend comes, in large part, from other people. From other customers' deposits, from investment funds, from capital waiting to be moved. That means the bank needs to lend it to make a profit. It doesn't want money sitting still. It wants to move it, to multiply it. And if you give it a good reason to do it with you, it will.

But that reason must be accompanied by a plan. It's not enough to want money; you have to know what you're going to use it for and how you're going to repay it.

That's why financial education is key. You don't need to be an expert in economics, but you do need to understand basic concepts: what an interest rate is, what long-term credit means, and the difference between good debt and bad debt. You need to know how to read bank statements, understand your income and expenses, and calculate whether an investment is truly worthwhile. When you manage this information, banking ceases to be a mystery. It becomes predictable, manageable, and useful. It becomes a powerful tool in your hands.

And here comes the most interesting part: once you manage to use the bank to your advantage once, everything becomes easier. If you invested well in a loan and repaid it without problem, the bank will offer you more. If you showed results, they will offer you better terms. And then growth accelerates. You no longer depend solely on your money, or your physical effort. Now you have a powerful institution that supports you, that finances you, that gives you access to capital. And that's what the rich do. They don't keep their money, they move it. They don't fear banks, they use them.

In short, making the bank work for you is possible, but it requires you to stop seeing it as simply a place where you keep your money. It's an institution designed to move money, to lend it, to make it grow. If you position yourself as someone who can use that money wisely, then the bank will seek you out. It will offer you products, open doors for you, treat you like a partner. And when that happens, you are no longer just a person who serves the bank. The bank starts serving you. And that's where the real money game begins.

Smart Credit

When most people hear the word "credit," the first thing they think of is debt, problems, monthly payments, and interest that eats you alive. And while that can happen if used incorrectly, the reality is that credit is a powerful tool, one of the greatest tools available for financial growth. The problem isn't credit itself; it's the lack of education on how to use it wisely. Misused credit can sink you. But well-used credit can propel you to the next level. It can be the lever you need to multiply your money, accelerate your path, and build wealth faster than you could with savings alone.

So, what is smart credit? It's credit you take out with a clear purpose, with a plan behind it, and repaid painlessly because it generates more money than it costs. It's literally using the bank's money to work for you. For example, taking out credit to buy a television or go on vacation may give you momentary satisfaction, but that's not smart credit. It's emotional credit, impulsive credit, consumer credit. It leaves you with nothing but a hanging debt and an excitement that fades within weeks. On the other hand, smart credit is credit you use to invest in something that pays you back, every month or in the near future.

Let's see this with a practical example. Imagine you have the opportunity to buy a machine that produces a product you can sell. It costs one thousand dollars. You don't have any savings, but you know that machine can generate two hundred dollars a month in sales. The bank offers you a loan with installments of one hundred dollars a month. You take it, buy the machine, produce, sell, pay the installment, and you're left with one hundred dollars in profit every month. When you finish paying, the machine still belongs to you, and those two hundred dollars a month are now completely yours. In that scenario, you used the loan as an investment, not as an expense. Those are the kinds of decisions that build wealth.

Another way to use credit intelligently is to leverage the real estate market. Real estate is one of the safest and most solid vehicles for generating passive income and building wealth. Let's say you find a well-priced apartment that you can rent. The bank lends you the money to buy it, you put down a down payment, and each month you pay the loan installment with the same money the tenant gives you. You're not contributing anything out of your own pocket, but you're gaining ownership, generating income, and taking advantage of the property's appreciation. You're using credit as a ladder that allows you to climb the ladder without having to make all the effort yourself.

Now, smart credit isn't just about what you use it for, it's also about how you negotiate it. Many people accept the bank's terms without question. They don't ask for better rates, they don't compare offers, they don't fully understand the terms. But banks are businesses, not charities. They want to lend to you, but they'll do so under their rules, unless you know how to play the game. Learn to compare interest rates, review the type of credit that best suits you based on the term, amount, and purpose. If it's for a business, look for commercial loans. If it's for a real estate investment, negotiate a fixed-rate mortgage. All of this makes the difference between making money or drowning in payments.

Smart credit also has to do with the timing. It's not about living in debt all the time; it's about choosing the right moment. Don't take out a loan when you're in crisis, desperate, or without plans. That's the worst time. The best time is when you already have an opportunity in the works, when you've done the math, when you can clearly see how the loan will benefit you, and how you'll repay it without problems. It's like riding a bike downhill: speed helps. But if you ride uphill and gasp for air, you'll only tire faster.

It's also important to understand that credit shouldn't be used as a magic bullet. It's not an instant savior. It won't change your life on its own. It's a tool, and like any tool, it works if you use it well. A hammer can build a house or it can destroy a window. The same goes for credit. If you use it intelligently, strategically, with vision, it can build you wealth, a business, a new financial life. But if you use it impulsively, without calculation, without knowledge, it can destroy your peace of mind, your reputation, and your ability to grow.

That's why it's vital that before applying for any loan, you ask yourself some key questions. Why do I want this money? Will this earn me more than it costs? Can I pay it off without compromising my personal finances? Am I investing or just buying out of desire? If the answers are clear and positive, then you're looking at a good loan opportunity. If they aren't, wait. Learn more. Adjust your plan. Or simply don't take out the loan. Because sometimes, the smartest loan is the one you decide not to use.

Finally, there's a powerful idea you should always remember: rich people aren't afraid of credit; they master it. They know how to use it as a lever to grow, to earn more, to advance faster. Poor people, on the other hand, tend to use credit to survive, to fill gaps, to consume what they can't afford. This difference in mindset is the key to everything. It's not how much you earn; it's how you use what you have. If you learn to use credit intelligently, purposefully, and strategically, bank money won't be a burden, it'll be an ally. And when credit works for you, the path to financial freedom shortens, accelerates, and becomes real.

The Bank Leverage Formula to Multiply Your Wealth

Increasing your wealth doesn't have to be a distant dream, reserved only for the wealthy. In fact, there's a clear, logical, and powerful formula that many people don't know or dare to use: bank leverage. And although it sounds complicated, it isn't. It's simply using the bank's money, instead of your own, to acquire assets that increase in value or generate income. In other words, it's growing faster without having to put everything out of your own pocket. It's like standing on the shoulders of a giant to achieve what, on your own, would take you years to accomplish.

The key is to understand that banks are full of money. Money that isn't theirs. It belongs to their clients, but they lend it as if it were their own. That money is looking to be invested. Banks lend it and charge interest on it. You can be one of those recipients, not to waste it, but to make it earn you more money than it costs you. That's the basis of leverage: using good debt to acquire good assets.

Let's imagine a simple example. Let's say you have ten thousand dollars saved. You can use that money to buy something with cash. But if you use that money as a down payment to ask the bank for a loan of ninety thousand more dollars, you now have one hundred thousand dollars to invest. With that one hundred thousand, you can buy an income property, or even two small ones. Those properties generate income every month, pay off the loan, and still leave you with some profit. And over the years, the properties increase in value. When you finish paying the bank, you keep the entire asset. Your initial investment was ten thousand, but now you have equity worth much more. That's multiplication.

That's the formula: little equity plus good debt equals equity multiplication. But the key is to have good debt. That is, it must be well calculated, you can easily repay it, and it must be backed by an asset that generates money or increases in value over time. People who don't understand this think that debt is bad. And yes, going into debt to buy things that depreciate or don't generate anything is a trap. But going into debt to acquire assets is a growth strategy. It's what great entrepreneurs, successful investors, even people who have built empires from scratch do.

Most people work their entire lives to save and buy things little by little. They do it without leverage. It's a slow path, full of effort and sacrifice. But those who understand the game of leverage go faster. Because they don't work only with their own money. They use other people's money. Of course, it's not about going into debt for the sake of it. It's about having a strategic mind. It's like playing chess with money. Every move has to be thought out so that the debt works for you, not the other way around.

Bank leverage can also be applied to business. Let's say you have a solid business idea, a clear and well-structured plan, but you lack the initial capital. You can present your project to the bank, ask for a loan, and get started. If the business does well, what you earn covers the bank's payments and leaves you with a profit. You've used the bank's money as a driving force. And when you finish paying it off, the business is yours, without having invested all the initial capital out of your own pocket.

Another way leverage multiplies your wealth is through the concept of appreciation. When you buy real estate with a loan, you pay part of the money and the bank pays the rest. But over time, the asset's value can increase significantly. Suppose you bought a property for $100,000 with a down payment of $20,000, and five years later that property is worth $150,000. That increase in value wasn't on your $20,000, it was on the $100,000. In other words, you multiplied your original investment without having to pay everything out of pocket. That growth is called return on invested capital, and when you use leverage, that return skyrockets.

Of course, we mustn't forget that leverage has two sides. Just as it can make you grow faster, it can also amplify mistakes. That's why it's vital to do the math right, understand the risks, have a contingency plan, and not fall in love with any investment without first evaluating it carefully. Leverage works if you maintain control. It's not about gambling, but about calculating. It's not about taking unnecessary risks, but about using financial logic to your advantage.

Banks are willing to lend you money if you provide them with security. Security that you know what you're doing, that you have the means to repay, that the asset backs the loan. Therefore, being well prepared, educating yourself, and knowing how to present a good proposal is an essential part of the process. It's not just asking for the sake of asking. It's showing that you understand the game. That you're not just another client, but a strategic partner who will make good use of the capital.

The formula for bank leverage is there, within everyone's reach. But few see it. Few dare to use it. Because many still think it's better not to owe anything, that it's safer to take things step by step, without risks. But true growth requires courage, intelligence, and strategy. If you learn to use bank money as your ally, as your springboard, you can climb higher and faster than most. You don't need to be a millionaire to get started. You just need to understand the formula, respect the rules of the game, and have the courage to act with a cool head and clear vision.

The money is circulating. The bank has it. Someone is going to use it. The question is: will you use it to multiply your wealth, or will you let someone else use it while you continue waiting? Leverage isn't for everyone, but it is for those who think differently, for those who understand that financial freedom isn't achieved through effort alone, but also through strategy. That's the difference between working for money and making money work for you. That's the real formula.

How to Use Mortgages, Leases, and Business Loans to Grow

One of the most powerful things you can learn in the world of finance is how to use the system's tools to your advantage. And three of the most useful tools available today are mortgages, leasing, and business loans. They're not just mechanisms for getting into debt, as many people think. They're keys. Keys that, if you know how to use them intelligently, can open the doors to accelerated growth, expansion, and the creation of real wealth. The problem is that most people are afraid of them because they don't understand them. And what isn't understood is rejected. But here we're going to unravel all that mystery so you can see the power before you.

Let's start with the mortgage. A mortgage is simply a large loan that a bank gives you to buy a property, usually a home, using the property itself as collateral. That is, the bank lends you the money, but if you don't pay, it keeps the property. Most people use mortgages to buy the house they'll live in, which is fine if done logically. But the wealthy use mortgages more strategically: to acquire income-generating properties. Instead of using their money to buy a house outright, they use it as a down payment to get a mortgage that allows them to buy several properties that they then rent out. With that rent, they pay the monthly payment and also earn positive cash flow. This way, they make the debt work for them.

For example, imagine you have $50,000. You could buy a small house with that money. But if you use it as a down payment, you could mortgage three rental apartments worth $100,000 each. Each one generates monthly income. The rent pays the mortgage, and you keep the asset. Over time, the apartments appreciate, the mortgages pay themselves off, and you end up with much greater wealth. That's the logic of a mortgage, used wisely: acquiring assets that pay for themselves and grow in value.

Now let's talk about leasing. Leasing is a type of rent-to-own arrangement. It's very common in the vehicle sector and also in capital goods, such as business machinery. Instead of buying something expensive outright, you rent it for a period of time, pay a monthly fee, and at the end, you can keep it by paying a residual value. It's a smart way to use an asset without committing much initial capital. This is useful for entrepreneurs and business owners who need vehicles or machinery but don't have or don't want to use all their money at once.

Imagine you own a construction company. Instead of buying a backhoe for $100,000, you lease it. You pay a small down payment and monthly installments while you use the machine. The money you earn from the jobs you do with that machine allows you to cover the installments. At the end of the contract, you can buy it back for a lower price. In other words, the asset has paid for itself thanks to the work it generated. This allows you to grow faster, have better tools, and compete at a different level, without having to commit your capital immediately.

Finally, there are commercial loans. These loans are designed for businesses. They are not personal or consumer loans. They are loans given to companies to grow, buy inventory, expand, hire staff, or acquire productive assets. The key here is to only take them out when the money will generate more money. It's not about borrowing to fill gaps, but rather borrowing to scale.

For example, if you have a restaurant and it's doing well, you can take out a business loan to open a second location. You use part of the loan to adapt the premises, hire staff, and purchase equipment. But you already have a proven model; you already know how to operate. The new location starts generating revenue. If you did it right, you pay off the loan without any problems and now have two restaurants instead of one. Your revenue has doubled, and your market presence has grown. That's commercial leverage.

Another smart way to use business loans is to purchase inventory in large quantities. Suppliers sometimes offer deep discounts if you buy in bulk. If you have access to credit, you can take advantage of that opportunity, buy cheap, sell at a good price, and make a good profit. What others can't do due to lack of capital, you can do because you know how to use business credit.

Now, for all these tools to work in your favor, one thing is essential: you need to have your finances in order and your banking profile clean. Banks don't lend to just anyone. You need to prove that you know how to manage money, that you have a stable income, and that you can repay. Having clear financial statements, a healthy credit history, and a well-structured plan makes all the difference. Having a good idea isn't enough; you have to prove it with numbers.

It's also important to understand that all of these tools have a cost. There's interest, there are fees, there are conditions. But if the money you earn from them allows you to generate more than it costs you, then the cost is an investment. This is where financial mindset comes in. You don't see interest as an expense, you see it as the price of an opportunity you wouldn't have without leverage.

Using mortgages, leasing, and commercial loans doesn't make you a slave to the bank. It makes you a partner, if you know how to manage it. The bank provides the money, you provide the strategy. And if both win, the system works. The problem arises when you borrow money without knowing what to do with it. When you take on debt to fill gaps, to show off, to spend on things that don't produce. But when debt is aimed at generating more value, more cash flow, more growth, then it becomes your best ally.

What you need to understand is that true growth often isn't achieved with your own resources alone. Other people's money, used wisely, can accelerate your path. And banks are full of money waiting to be borrowed. Leasing gives you tools you couldn't buy immediately. Mortgages give you access to properties that generate long-term wealth. And business loans give you the muscle to compete, innovate, and scale.

If you learn to use them with a cool head, clear numbers, and a vision for the future, you'll stop being someone afraid of going into debt and become someone who uses the system to build. Because the system already exists. It already works. You just need to learn to navigate it. And when you do it right, you don't just grow, you multiply. And you don't just build businesses, you build freedom.

The Art of Asking the Bank for Money (and Getting It)

Asking for money at a bank may seem simple. You walk in, apply for a loan, hand over some paperwork, and wait for a response. But the reality is very different. Asking for money from a bank and getting it isn't a matter of luck or friendliness. It's an art. A strategic process that blends preparation, perception, and presentation. If you don't do it right, they'll turn you away. But if you do it like a pro, they don't just lend you money; they respect you. Because banks, even if it doesn't seem like it, want to lend money. That's their way of making money. The problem is that they don't lend to just anyone. They want to, but only if they think they'll get it back, with interest. That's why learning how to ask for money intelligently is a skill that can make the difference between growth and stagnation.

The first step to getting a bank to lend you money is to understand that they're not doing you a favor. They're doing you a business. They make a profit if you pay them every installment, every month, with their well-calculated interest. The bank is a business. It doesn't feel. It doesn't care about your life story or your dreams. It cares about numbers, risk, and the likelihood that you'll repay what it gives you. If you can't speak their language, they don't understand you, and they won't lend to you. It's that simple.

So, the first thing you need is to build a good financial reputation. This starts long before you apply for a loan. In fact, it starts even before you need money. It means having active bank accounts, regular transactions, on-time payments, and zero overdue debts. Everything you do with your money is recorded, and banks analyze that behavior. If they see order, they consider you trustworthy. If they see chaos, they consider you risky. And believe me, banks hate risk.

Another key point is your credit history. This is like your resume in the world of money. Every loan, card, installment, service—everything counts. If you've ever missed a payment, that's shown. If you've always paid on time, it also counts. Having a good credit history opens doors for you. A bad credit history closes them without giving you the chance to explain yourself. So before you apply, check your credit history. Make sure it's clean and has a good score. If it isn't, your priority should be to fix it before you sit down with the banker.

Now comes the time to apply. This is where many people fail, not because they don't qualify, but because they don't know how to present their case well. Asking a bank for money is like presenting an investment project. You have to explain exactly what you want the money for, how you're going to use it, how much you expect to earn, and how you're going to pay. It's not enough to simply say "I want to open a business." That's not enough. You have to show the business, explain the costs, revenue, margins, cash flow, and payment plan. The clearer you are, the more trust you generate.

Imagine you want to open a coffee shop. Don't just say, "I want $100,000 for a space." Prepare a document that explains that you already have a location identified, how much the rent is, how much you'll invest in furniture, how much you expect to sell per day, what your margin per coffee sold will be, how you'll market yourself, who your competition is, what you do differently, what month you expect to start making a profit, and when you'll repay the money. That's what the bank wants to see: clarity, data, control, accountability.

A very important tip is not to ask for more money than you really need. Many people believe that asking for more will make them look ambitious or important, but it actually raises doubts. The bank doesn't want to give you extra money to keep or misuse. It wants to know that every dollar it asks for has a justifiable purpose. If you need 80,000,000, don't ask for 100,000 just in case. Ask for 80,000 and explain why that's the right amount. That speaks to control and good management.

Another point that banks value highly is your own capital. When you also contribute money to the project, the bank understands that you're taking a risk. That you have something to lose. That gives them security. They don't want to lend to someone who has nothing at stake. If you risk your own money, the bank feels more comfortable lending you theirs. So, if you can, always contribute a portion of the capital. That makes you appear more committed and more solid.

Personal presentation also counts, even if no one says so openly. If you arrive at the bank disorganized, without paperwork, unclear, or unprepared, your ideas don't matter. They see you as an improviser. But if you arrive with a well-prepared folder, all your documents ready, a printed plan, and even a short presentation, you're already above average. Most people don't even know what they're going to say. You, on the other hand, arrive as a professional. And banks prefer to deal with professionals.

Also remember that every loan is a negotiation. Don't settle for the first offer. Ask about rates, terms, fees, and insurance. Banks don't usually explain everything. You have to ask. Sometimes you can improve a rate simply by negotiating. Or you can get better terms if you show you have other options. Don't present yourself as someone in need, but as someone with a solid project and looking for the right partner. That changes everything.

And if for some reason they say no, don't give up. Ask them to explain why. Learn. Improve. Adjust your profile and try again.

Many successful entrepreneurs were rejected the first time. But they didn't give up. They improved their track record, better prepared their proposal, and came back stronger. Asking the bank for money is like training a muscle. The more you do it, the better you get. All you need is information, strategy, and determination.

The bank isn't your enemy. It's a tool. And like any tool, if you use it well, it can help you build great things. But it's not enough to just want it. You have to know how to play the game. And in this game, the one who is best prepared wins. So be prepared. Learn the art. Because when you know how to ask, they don't just lend you money; they open doors. And those doors can take you exactly where you want to go.

The Strategy of the Rich

When you look at the truly wealthy, those with businesses, properties, and investments everywhere, you often think it all started with a large inheritance or a stroke of luck. But what very few people see is the strategy behind that growth. Most of the wealthy didn't get rich by working hard or saving every penny. They got rich because they learned how to manage their money intelligently. They knew how to use other people's resources, especially bank money, to multiply their wealth without necessarily having all the money in their pockets. And that strategy isn't magic; it's knowledge applied time and again, with discipline and a long-term vision.

The rich don't fear debt. They understand it, analyze it, and use it to their advantage. While many see a loan as a burden, they see it as leverage. If someone wants to buy a million-dollar property, most people think about saving until they have a million. But the rich think about putting down only 20 percent, and having the bank cover the rest. And with that property, they generate income that pays off the loan, the taxes, and also leaves a profit. The rich don't decapitalize themselves or wait 20 years to have the money. They leverage themselves, buy now, and let the system work for them.

The strategy of the wealthy is based on three fundamental pillars: using other people's money, creating assets that generate cash flow, and repeating the process. Each step is carefully thought out so that the money works and doesn't stagnate. For example, when they take out a loan, they don't use it to buy things that lose value, like a luxury car or expensive clothes. They use it to buy assets that generate money: real estate, businesses, machinery, dividend-paying stocks, or even financial products that multiply over time. What they buy generates money, and that money pays off the debt. Thus, they not only preserve their initial capital, but each asset they acquire allows them to have more cash flow to acquire another. It's a chain.

Another very important detail is how the wealthy protect themselves. They don't do everything in their own name. They use companies, partnerships, and trusts. Not because they want to hide, but because they understand that wealth must be protected. If you have property in your name and someone sues you, they can take it away. But if it's in the name of a company, it's more difficult. Furthermore, by having business structures, they can access larger commercial loans, at lower rates, and with more tax benefits. The wealthy don't improvise. They have legal and accounting teams advising them, and every move is designed to minimize risks and maximize profits.

One point many overlook is that the rich also know when not to use their money. If someone offers them a great opportunity, they don't rush to empty their account. They seek financing, convince others to invest with them, and grow with third-party resources. In other words, they don't use their own money when they can use someone else's. This isn't greed, it's strategy. Because while others use everything they have for a single move, they make five different moves with borrowed money, well controlled and well planned. This way they grow much faster and diversify their risks.

Furthermore, the wealthy view time differently. The average person looks for immediate results. If they invest something today, they want to see a profit next week. But the wealthy invest with years in mind. They know that a property can double in value in ten years, that a business needs time to grow, that a good financial deal can improve with inflation. They think like farmers, not hunters. They plant now, water carefully, and wait for the harvest. This allows them to make more solid moves, with less anxiety, and with greater foresight.

Another essential part of their strategy is that they don't live below their means, but they don't live for show either. Most of the wealthy who use leverage well aren't the ones you see on social media with expensive watches and exotic cars. They're those who live comfortably, yes, but who devote much of their energy to continuing to grow their wealth. They know that their true luxury isn't spending money, but rather having financial freedom, not having to work if they don't want to, knowing that their investments generate income even while they sleep.

And the most curious thing is that many rich people don't even earn more money than the middle class in terms of salary. The difference lies in what they do with that money. The middle class tends to spend it on liabilities: their own house, a new car, vacations on credit. The rich invest it in assets. If they earn ten thousand dollars, they look to turn five thousand into something that generates another five hundred a month. And so, over time, those small steps become a solid structure, which grows on its own, like a well-oiled machine.

The strategy of the rich isn't secret. It's plain to see. The problem is that many don't want to or don't know how to see it. It requires discipline, patience, study, and a different mindset. It's not for those who want quick results or those who fear risk. It's for those who understand that financial freedom is built with intelligence, not luck. And that money, well managed, can be a silent employee that works for you every day, without complaint or rest.

If you want to apply the strategy of the rich, you don't need to be a millionaire. You need to think like them. Learn their rules, apply their methods, and make decisions that gradually bring you closer to that way of life. Because the most powerful thing the rich have isn't money. It's the way they think. And that, if you want, can also be yours. You just have to start acting differently, think about assets, use leverage intelligently, and never stop learning. Because wealth isn't about how much you have, but how you grow it.

Rates, Terms and Types of Credit

When a person approaches a bank to borrow money, they face three elements that seem simple, but are fundamental to determining whether the loan will be a springboard to growth or a chain around their neck: the interest rate, the loan term, and the type of loan they are requesting. These three concepts determine how much they will repay, for how long, and how smart or dangerous their financial decision is. Understanding them isn't complicated, but it's key to avoiding traps disguised as opportunities.

The interest rate is, simply put, the price you pay for using money that isn't yours. It's what the bank earns by lending it to you. If you borrow ten thousand dollars at an annual interest rate of ten percent, that means that after a year, you will have paid one thousand dollars just for the use of the money, in addition to the original amount you must repay. Now, many people don't notice this detail, or they see it as something minor, but a poorly understood interest rate can eat into your profits and turn a profitable investment into a financial disaster. That's why it's vital to compare them, understand whether they are fixed or variable, and calculate how they will behave over time.

A fixed rate is one that doesn't change over the term of the loan. What you pay today will be the same as what you'll pay in five or ten years. It's predictable and easy to plan for. A variable rate, on the other hand, can change over time, depending on market conditions, inflation, or monetary policy. It may be low today, but in a couple of years it can double, and that can skyrocket your monthly payments. Many mortgages or business loans offer variable rates at the start, with the enticement that they're lower. But if you don't understand this change, you could end up paying much more than you thought.

The second key point is the term. The term is the time you're given to repay the money. The longer the term, the smaller the monthly payments, but the more interest you pay overall. The shorter the term, the higher the payments, but you end up paying less interest. Here's the trick: many people are lured into the lower payment because it seems more convenient, but they don't realize that this means they'll be paying interest for more years, and that in the end they'll have paid almost double what they borrowed. For example, a 30-year mortgage may seem light monthly, but if you compare it with a 15-year mortgage, the difference in what you end up paying can be huge.

Therefore, when you think about the term, don't just think about how much you can pay today, but also how much you want to pay in total. A business owner who understands finance always seeks to shorten terms, even if the installments are higher, because they know this frees up their cash flow in the future and pays less to the bank. Furthermore, the faster you pay off a loan, the faster you can take out another one to continue growing.

Now let's talk about the type of loan. Not all loans are the same. There are personal loans, mortgage loans, business loans, leasing, lines of credit, among others. Each has its own purpose, terms, and structure. A personal loan, for example, is quick and without many requirements, but it usually has higher interest rates because the bank assumes more risk. It's ideal for an emergency or a one-time expense, but not for financing a business or a long-term investment.

Mortgage loans are specifically designed for property purchases. They offer lower rates and longer terms because the property is used as collateral. This type of loan is ideal if you plan to invest in real estate. But you must be careful not to pay more for the property than it's actually worth, or to get into mortgages with unclear terms. You should always consider the total cost, not just the monthly payment.

Commercial loans are for businesses. They can be used to purchase machinery, hire staff, expand operations, or invest in inventory. These loans can be larger and have flexible terms, but they require proof that the business generates stable income. This is where banks want to see projections, financial statements, and cash flow. If you can present your business professionally, you can access better amounts and better rates.

There's also leasing, which is a type of rent-to-own arrangement. It's widely used for vehicles or machinery. You don't buy the asset outright, but instead use it for a fee, and at the end, you can buy it for a residual value. It's useful if you don't want to make a large initial investment but need the equipment right away. In many countries, leasing has tax advantages because you can deduct it as an operating expense. Wealthy people use it all the time so they don't tie up their money.

Another very interesting product is the line of credit. It's not a loan as such, but rather a limit of money that the bank gives you to use whenever you need it. You only pay interest on the money you actually use, not on the entire approved amount. It's like a credit card, but in a business or personal format. Having a line of credit available gives you peace of mind and flexibility. It helps you cover unexpected expenses, take advantage of quick opportunities, or maintain liquidity without having to take out a new loan each time.

Each type of credit has its place, and it's not a question of which is best, but rather which is best suited for what you're trying to achieve. A common mistake is using a type of credit for something it wasn't designed for. For example, using a high-interest personal loan to finance a long-term real estate investment, or using a credit card to cover operating expenses for an uncontrolled business. That only leads to a snowball effect that's difficult to manage.

The most important thing in all of this is to understand that credit isn't bad. It's a tool. What can be bad is how you use it. If you know the rates, choose the right term, and use the right type of credit for your goals, then you're using the financial system to your advantage. You're playing by the rules of the big boys. But if you make thoughtless decisions, guided only by necessity or the emotion of the moment, you end up trapped in a cycle of debt that robs you of freedom.

In short, every time you're ready to take out a loan, ask yourself these questions: How much am I actually going to pay, including interest? What's the shortest term I can afford without drowning? Am I using the right type of loan for my goal? If you answer clearly, you'll be making a conscious decision. And that, in the world of money, is what makes the difference between moving forward and stagnating. Because banks are there to lend, but you're the one who decides whether the loan pushes you up or drags you down.

How to Boost Your Credit Profile Like a Millionaire Entrepreneur

Having a good credit profile is like having a brilliant resume in the financial world. It's what banks see when you decide to borrow money. If your profile is weak, messy, or shows you don't know how to manage debt, they'll turn you down or lend you little at sky-high interest rates. But if your profile is as fat as that of a millionaire entrepreneur, banks will seek you out, offer you special terms, and open lines of credit that you can use to multiply your wealth. The trick is to build that profile with strategy, patience, and a lot of intelligence.

To begin with, you need to understand that your credit history is a reflection of how you handle other people's money. It doesn't matter if you have millions in cash stashed under your mattress. If you've never taken out a loan, you don't exist to the bank. And if you've borrowed and repaid poorly, you do exist, but as a risky client. The good news is that anyone, even starting from scratch, can build a solid profile in just a few years if they follow the right steps. And the best part is, you don't need a lot of money, just discipline and vision.

The first step to building credit is to start building credit. Many people think the best thing to do is avoid debt, never use a credit card, and live on cash alone. But that doesn't build credit. It's like trying to build muscle without ever going to the gym. To build a good credit history, you have to use credit, even if you don't need it. Open a credit card, use it for your regular expenses, and pay it off on time. Do this every month. It's not about going into debt, but about showing that you know how to use credit and that you're trustworthy. This routine is like lifting weights for your credit score.

Now, it's not just about having one card. It's about having several different credit accounts and managing them well. Banks look at your credit mix. They want to see that you manage cards, loans, maybe an auto loan or a mortgage, and that you pay on time everywhere. This tells them that you not only know how to manage a small debt, but that you're also capable of managing several at the same time without problems. This diversity strengthens your profile as an entrepreneur. You're not someone who's just making a living, but someone who knows how to play the financial game.

A millionaire entrepreneur not only has personal credit, but also business credit. And that's a very important step. You have to separate your personal finances from those of your business. Create a legally constituted company. Register it, open a bank account in the company's name, and start generating business from there. Even if you manage everything alone at first, from the bank's perspective, you're already a separate entity, and that gives you access to a whole new world of credit.

Once you have your business legally and operational, start applying for small loans in your company's name. You can open a business card or request a small line of credit. Pay it off on time. Repeat the process several times, and in a few months, your company will begin to have its own credit history. The bank now sees not only your personal profile but also your business's. And if both are solid, the opportunities multiply. It's like having two arms to carry money, instead of one.

Also, something that very few people do but that has a lot of weight on your profile is strategically requesting credit line increases. If you have a card with a thousand-dollar limit and you use it well for a few months, ask the bank to raise your limit. They'll do so if they see you're a good payer. You don't need to use all of that new limit, but having it available improves your utilization ratio, which is one of the key factors in your credit score. The more credit you have available and the less you use, the better your profile looks. It's like having an entire stadium to yourself and only using a corner of it. That's impressive.

Another detail that makes a big difference is time. The age of your accounts is also important. That's why never close your oldest cards, even if you no longer use them. Keeping them open shows the bank that you've had a solid financial relationship for years. If you close old accounts, you shorten your credit history and can lose points. The same goes for your business accounts. Keep them active, make changes, even if they're small. The bank wants to see life, movement, and consistency.

A little-known but very powerful technique is to become an authorized user on a card with a good credit history. If you have a family member or friend with an older, well-managed card and a good limit, ask them to add you as an authorized user. That account will appear on your history as if it were yours, and you'll inherit its age and good behavior. You don't need to use it; just be there. It's a quick way to give your credit profile a serious boost, especially if you're just starting out.

Finally, don't forget to monitor your credit history. Many errors appear there without you even realizing it: incorrectly recorded payments, accounts that don't belong to you, or outdated information. Review your report at least once a year and dispute any errors you find. Take care of your credit history like you take care of your reputation, because it depends on whether the bank sees you as a regular customer or as a millionaire construction entrepreneur.

Building a strong credit profile isn't a matter of luck or having millions. It's a strategy. Start small, but with a vision for the big picture.

Use credit, not to spend, but to show you know how to manage it. Separate your personal and business finances. Diversify your credit products. Ask for line increases. Maintain your seniority. Become an authorized user. And review your reports. Do this for a year or two, and you'll be amazed at how it changes the way banks view you. They'll no longer see you as someone who needs help. They'll see you as a strategic partner. And when banks want to partner with you, you're one step away from playing in the big leagues.

The Infinite Money Strategy

Imagine having a source of money that never runs out. Not because you have millions stashed away, but because you know how to make that money come back to you again and again, like a boomerang. That's the infinite money strategy. It's not magic, nor a myth reserved for billionaires; it's a smart and structured way to use other people's money, especially bank money, to steadily grow your wealth. This strategy is so powerful that those who understand it no longer think about saving money, but rather about how to move it, use it, multiply it, and get it back, again and again.

The foundation of everything is understanding that money isn't meant to stay still. Money is like water: if it stagnates, it rots; if it flows, it gives life. The money you keep in the bank, sitting idle, loses value every day due to inflation. But if that money is invested strategically, it can generate more money, which in turn can be reinvested. Thus begins the cycle. And the best part is, you don't even have to use your own money to start this system. You can use the bank's money, pay it back, and keep the profit.

That's leverage. And when done right, it's the formula for infinite money.

The secret is to create a closed system where money comes in, multiplies, and then returns to the same point to start over. One of the best examples of this strategy is the world of real estate. Let's say you buy a property using a bank loan. You put down a small down payment, and the bank lends you the rest. You fix up the property, rent it out, and generate monthly income. With that income, you pay the bank's installment and still have a profit. After a while, that property increases in value. You refinance—that is, you take out a new loan based on the current value, take out a portion in cash, and with that money, buy another property. You repeat the process. And now you have two assets generating cash flow. That's money coming back, reinvesting, and multiplying.

What few people understand is that in this game, initial capital is recycled. You don't have to start from scratch every time. The same money you put in once can go around indefinitely if you know how to use it. The important thing is not to take money out to spend on luxuries or whims, but to always reinvest it in assets that generate more income. That's why it's called infinite money. Because, in theory, it never stops. One property leads to another. A well-structured business leads to another. One profitable investment feeds the next. Everything feeds back, like a machine that never stops working.

Another very powerful example is using a line of credit to finance a quick business opportunity. Let's say you see a wholesale product purchase that you can resell for triple the price in a few days. You use a bank line of credit to make the purchase, sell quickly, pay the bank back, and keep the profit. That profit isn't debt. It's yours. And if you repeat this cycle many times a year, you can generate large sums without having invested a single cent of your own. It's speed, intelligence, and strategy. The money doesn't have to be yours to work in your favor.

This strategy also works in the business world. Successful entrepreneurs don't fund their businesses with their own money. They look for investors, banks, and financial partners. The important thing is that the business works, that it generates cash flow, that it can be scaled. If you can demonstrate to the bank that the money they lend you will generate solid, sufficient income to repay it and also leave a profit, there's no reason for them to deny you a loan. They want to lend you money because you earn them interest. But you earn more because the bank's money made you money without ever having had any.

In this formula, it's key to understand that time and trust are everything. You can't expect to apply the infinite money strategy if you don't have financial order, if you don't pay on time, if you don't understand the terms, interest rates, and risks. You need to build a good relationship with banks, have a track record, and demonstrate that you know how to manage credit. That reputation gives you access to better terms, larger lines of credit, and more lucrative opportunities. And the larger your financial network, the more money you can move without having to use your own.

Now, you have to be careful. It's not about senselessly going into debt or getting involved in dubious projects. Infinite money only works if the flow is constant. Income must be greater than expenses. Always. Every loan must be backed by a real source of income to repay it. If you stray from this principle, the system collapses. That's why financial education is so important. You can't apply this strategy if you don't know exactly how money works, how banks operate, how to evaluate an investment, or how to calculate your return.

The infinite money strategy is, in essence, a way of thinking. It's about stopping seeing money as an object to be stored and starting to see it as a tool to be moved. It's about thinking like an entrepreneur, not a consumer. It's about using the system to your advantage, understanding its rules, and playing smart. It's about understanding that the most powerful money isn't the money you have, but the money you know how to ask for, manage, and multiply.

Once you master this way of thinking, your life changes. You no longer dream of saving for years to buy one house. You think about how to finance five houses in five years. You're no longer so concerned with earning more money, but rather with finding assets that work for you. You're no longer afraid to ask for money, because you know exactly what to do with it. And when you reach that point, money ceases to be a problem. It becomes a partner. And that partner, if you know how to treat them well, never tires of working for you. This is how truly infinite money is built.

Private Banking and Hidden Opportunities

When people think of a bank, they usually imagine a branch with a long line, a teller window, and someone depositing money or paying a bill. But what almost no one sees is that, behind that public facade, there is a completely different world. A silent, reserved, and exclusive world, where there are no lines, where customers don't need to ask permission to be served, and where money moves according to a different logic. This world is called private banking, and it's where banks truly demonstrate their power and their most sophisticated strategy. Private banking is like a VIP club where access depends on wealth, financial profile, and, above all, your potential to move money profitably.

The interesting thing is that you don't need to be a billionaire to knock on that door. In many cases, you just need to prove you know what you're doing with your money. Banks don't just look for large fortunes; they also look for entrepreneurially minded clients, people on the path to growth, with solid projects and ambition. Private banking is designed to help you multiply your money, but they also make money, so their interest is in your growth. If you grow, they grow too. That's the unwritten rule.

In traditional banking, you're just another client. In private banking, you're treated like a partner. The language changes, the service is personalized, and you're assigned a dedicated advisor who understands your business, your plans, and your goals. This advisor isn't just there to help you move your money, but also to introduce you to opportunities that aren't available in traditional banking. They tell you about alternative investments, customized portfolios, private projects, and off-the-radar options. Many of the world's best financial opportunities aren't advertised to the public, but circulate in this closed world, where relationships, information, and discretion are protected.

One of the great advantages of being in private banking is early access to investments. For example, there are real estate funds, private bonds, or technology startups that are open only to certain investors. You won't see this on a website or in an advertisement. Your advisor tells you about it because they know it's an opportunity that suits you. The bank offers you early access, even with special conditions. Why? Because they know you have the ability, track record, and vision. They know you're not a fearful saver, but a wealth builder.

In addition, private banking allows you to access much more flexible and powerful loans. While traditional banks require documentation, guarantees, and explanations, and often reject you for minor details, private banking operates with a different logic. They already know your profile. They already know how you manage risk. Loans are often approved based on trust and track record, rather than strict rules. You can obtain multimillion-dollar lines of credit with preferential rates, special terms, and customized structures. This gives you a huge competitive advantage. It allows you to move quickly when a good opportunity arises, without relying on slow and bureaucratic processes.

Another powerful advantage is wealth planning. Private banking not only helps you invest, but also teaches you how to protect and organize your assets. They help you create legal and tax structures that allow you to optimize taxes, protect your assets, plan inheritances, and distribute your wealth intelligently. This is key if you're building a large business, owning property, or thinking about expanding internationally. It's not enough to just make money. You have to learn how to conserve it and put it to work with smart rules. And that knowledge resides within private banking, not outside it.

Now, many are wondering how to get there. How do you go from being an ordinary customer to being part of that exclusive world? The first step is to have an investor mindset. Stop thinking like a consumer. Start organizing your money like a business. Keep your accounts clear, your taxes up to date, and your credits clean. Build relationships with banks, not just to borrow money, but to show your potential. If you have a business, present it as a serious project. If you have investments, document your returns well. If you use credit, use it to grow, not to survive. Before long, if you do things right, the bank will take notice. They'll call you. They'll invite you to a special meeting. Or, if you're more proactive, you can ask to be evaluated for private banking yourself. Not everyone qualifies, but if you do, doors open.

You also have to understand that private banking works largely by referral. Relationships are worth gold. If you know someone who's already in the business, ask them for an introduction. If you work with an accountant, lawyer, or financial advisor, ask if they have any connections to that industry. Sometimes, a good referral opens the door faster than a million pesos in your bank account. Because in that world, what counts isn't just money, but trust.

Therefore, don't underestimate the value of educating yourself, presenting yourself well, and having a long-term vision. Private banking is a powerful tool, but it's not for those who want to get rich quick. It's for those who want to grow intelligently, protect what they build, and multiply it without exposing it to unnecessary risks. It's a game of strategy, relationships, and insider information.

In short, private banking isn't an unattainable myth. It's a real opportunity available to anyone willing to prepare, play their cards right, and build a solid relationship with the financial system. Within that world, there are tools, resources, and opportunities that can completely change the speed of your economic growth. You don't need to be a millionaire to get in. But you do need to think like one. Because in private banking, you don't just handle money. You handle power. And if you know how to use it, that power can be on your side.

Fatal Mistakes When Using Bank Money

When you learn you can use bank money to grow, emotion can cloud judgment. It's easy to think you're in control just because you've secured a line of credit, a loan, or a mortgage. But this is where many stumble. Using bank money without a strategy, knowledge, or a clear vision can be like driving a Ferrari without knowing how to brake. Instead of moving toward wealth, many end up hitting a wall of debt, interest, and financial stress. That's why it's key to understand the most common mistakes people make when using bank money. Mistakes that seem small at first, but over time, become deadly traps.

The first fatal mistake is using bank money for things that don't generate a return. That is, to buy things that depreciate in value or that only satisfy a momentary desire. For example, taking out a loan to replace your cell phone, buy a new television, take a trip, or even pay off other debts. That's using bad debt. When you use borrowed money to consume, you're mortgaging your future for something that won't pay you back. And the worst part is that you pay for that luxury with interest. It's as if you were buying the same product, but two or three times more expensive, simply because you weren't patient or didn't plan well.

The second serious mistake is not understanding the loan terms. Many people sign without reading. Or they read, but don't understand. Or they understand, but don't ask questions. And then they're surprised to see that the installments increase, that the interest rates are variable, or that there are hidden fees. Before accepting money from the bank, you have to study everything carefully. Know if the interest rate is fixed or variable. Understand what happens if you're late. Know if there are penalties for paying early. Some loans have conditions disguised as opportunities. What seems easy at first can become a heavy burden over time. And that's when there's no turning back.

Another common mistake is relying too heavily on borrowed money. That is, building your entire business, your life, or your plans with other people's money. Leverage is a powerful tool, yes, but it must be used with balance. If everything you have is from the bank, you really have nothing. If your business only works because you're using debt to keep it alive, then you're standing on a ticking time bomb. A change in the market, an increase in interest rates, or a drop in your income can cause everything to collapse. And when that happens, the bank won't embrace you. It will charge you. And if you can't pay, it will take whatever you have.

We also have to mention the mistake of not having an exit plan. Many people borrow money without knowing exactly how they're going to repay it. They only think about the present, about getting what they want now, but they don't plan ahead. Every time you borrow money, you should be clear about how you're going to multiply it and how you're going to repay it. If you don't have a realistic, detailed plan, measured in time and numbers, then you're not using the bank's money. You're playing with fire. And sooner or later you're going to get burned.

Another very common mistake is not separating personal and business finances. This is typical of small business owners who mix their personal and business accounts. They borrow money for the business, but use it to pay personal expenses. Or, conversely, they go into personal debt to cover gaps in the business. This creates a mess that impedes growth and generates financial confusion. Furthermore, when it comes time to apply to the bank for a new loan, your profile looks weak because they can't understand how you really manage your money. Having organized and separate finances is a sign of financial maturity. Without this, it's difficult for a bank to take you seriously in the long term.

There's also the mistake of growing too quickly just because the bank lent you a loan. Some people receive a large line of credit and feel like they have a gold mine in their hands. They expand uncontrollably, hire more people, open new branches, and purchase expensive equipment, without yet having a solid foundation. This may seem like success, but it's actually inflated, artificial growth. And when sales aren't enough to cover expenses and pay off the debt, the castle collapses. You have to grow with strategy, not ego. The bank's money isn't there to inflate you, it's to leverage you intelligently.

Finally, one of the most destructive mistakes is not asking for help or advice. Many people think that using bank money is just a matter of signing and paying. But there's an art and science behind smart credit. There are financial advisors, accountants, and business consultants who can help you plan your debt use wisely. You can also learn on your own, read, study case studies, and analyze numbers. But if you don't do either of these things, then you're making important decisions with your eyes closed. And that's dangerous. Because the bank won't forgive you for your ignorance. If you can't pay, you'll face the consequences, whether you know how the system works or not.

Using bank money can be the lever that propels you to the next level. But it can also be the anchor that sinks you if you don't know how to manage it. It's not about being afraid of credit, but about respecting it. It's about understanding that it's a tool, not a reward. That it's designed to multiply your money if you use it with a cool head, clear vision, and discipline. Every time you make a financial decision, ask yourself: Is this going to give me more than it costs? Am I investing or am I buying a problem disguised as an opportunity? Am I growing or just pretending to grow?

Most fatal mistakes when using bank money come from not having a strategy, from acting on impulse, emotion, or ignorance. But if you take the time to learn, plan, and act intelligently, then credit ceases to be a risk and becomes an advantage. An advantage that very few know how to use well, but that you can master if you decide to do so with seriousness and commitment. Because in the world of money, those who win are not those who borrow the most, but those who know exactly what to do with what they borrow.

Become Your Own Bank

The idea of becoming your own bank may sound strange at first. After all, when you think of a bank, you imagine a huge building with marble columns, ATMs, suited executives, and vaults full of cash. But being your own bank has nothing to do with opening a branch or issuing credit cards. It's about taking complete control of your money. It means no longer relying on traditional banks every time you need capital. It means you can lend, you can invest, you can grow, using your own resources just like a financial institution would. And this isn't a fantasy or a romantic notion. It's a very real strategy used by smart people and successful entrepreneurs to build their wealth from the ground up.

To begin with, the first thing you need to understand is how the bank works with you. The bank takes your money, the money you deposit in your savings or checking account, and lends it to other people. It charges them interest. It gives you a small percentage of your savings, but charges the lender much more. That's their business: making money with other people's money. So, if you have money, and that money is just sitting there, motionless, doing nothing for you, then you're missing an opportunity. Your money needs to be moving, producing. That's what banks do, and that's what you can start doing on your own.

Becoming your own bank begins with a change of mindset. You no longer see your money as just something to spend. You see it as a tool to make more money. You begin to create a personal fund with a clear mission: to finance your own projects, invest in opportunities, and help you grow, instead of turning to an external bank. You don't need millions to do this. You can start with whatever you have. The important thing is to understand the principle: if instead of borrowing from a bank, you lend to yourself, you save the interest and multiply your wealth.

A very simple example. Imagine you need to buy a car for your business. You could go to the bank and ask for a loan. They'll lend you money, but they charge you interest, fees, and require collateral. In the end, that car costs you much more than it's worth. Now imagine that instead, you lend to yourself.

You've been building a personal fund for years, with discipline, and now you can take that money, buy the car, and then pay that money back into your own fund month by month, with interest if you want. You're acting as your own lender. Not only did you not lose on interest, but you maintained the discipline of paying that capital back to yourself, so you can continue using it in the future.

Being your own bank also means having a structure. It's not enough to just keep your money under your mattress. You need to organize it, assign goals, set rules, and treat it seriously. Some people open a separate account, exclusively for their "personal bank." They give that fund a name, define goals, and allocate a fixed percentage of their income to it each month. Little by little, that fund grows. And over time, you can use it to leverage investments, start businesses, cover emergencies, or simply to avoid resorting to expensive credit. Every time you use your fund, document it. You write down how much you took out, what you used it for, and how you're going to repay it. Because if you don't respect your own bank, no one else will.

An advanced form of this strategy is to use financial vehicles such as whole life insurance, investment accounts, or business structures that allow you to store capital in a tax-advantaged manner while still having access to that money when you need it. Some people in the United States, for example, use life insurance policies that accumulate cash value. This value can be borrowed by the owner, as if lending to themselves, and then returned to the fund. The money never left the system; it just changed uses for a time. Meanwhile, it continues to grow. This is a sophisticated way to bank yourself, and it's completely legal. The secret is to learn how the system works and use its rules to your advantage.

When you become your own bank, something changes in the way you view money. You no longer feel like a slave to banks. You no longer see debt as a necessity. You start thinking like a financial institution. You analyze risks. You evaluate returns. You make informed decisions, based on numbers, not impulses. Because now your money has a purpose, and you are the one who directs it. This not only gives you financial power, it also gives you mental freedom. You feel in control. And that's worth more than any approved credit card.

But be careful, being your own bank doesn't mean locking yourself in a box and never asking for a loan. It means having options. It means you can decide when to use the bank's money and when not. That you can negotiate from a position of strength. That you're not desperate for a loan because you have your own system. And when a big opportunity comes along, you can leverage it wisely. Because the bank isn't bad. The problem is using it without a strategy. And if you already have a solid foundation, then outside money can help you scale faster.

To achieve this, you need three things. The first is discipline. Because if you're not able to save consistently, you won't build anything. The second is education. You have to learn about finance, investments, basic accounting, taxes, and legal structures. You don't need to be an expert, but you do need to understand how money moves. And the third is vision. You have to know where you're going. What you want to build. Why you're accumulating that capital. If you don't have a clear goal, money is wasted on waste. But if you know what you want, your personal bank becomes your best ally.

The path to being your own bank isn't quick or easy. But it is possible, and more powerful than many imagine. It's an act of financial independence. It's a personal declaration that you're not going to keep asking for permission to grow. You're going to build your system. You're going to turn your money into a machine that works for you. And if you do it right, over time, you won't need to go to the bank anymore. The bank will come to you. Because they know when someone is mastering the game. And when you become your own bank, you don't just earn money. You gain respect, control, and above all, freedom.

www.ingramcontent.com/pod-product-compliance
Lightning Source LLC
LaVergne TN
LVHW090419210926
848480LV00002B/619